# HASHMAT EFFENDI

# Izza's Tea Party

## A Family Guide to
## Fire Safety and Burn Prevention

# Izza's Tea Party
## A Family Guide to Fire Safety and Burn Prevention

AuthorHouse™
1663 Liberty Drive
Bloomington, IN 47403
www.authorhouse.com
Phone: 833-262-8899

Because of the dynamic nature of the Internet, any web addresses or links contained in this book may have changed since publication and may no longer be valid. The views expressed in this work are solely those of the author and do not necessarily reflect the views of the publisher, and the publisher hereby disclaims any responsibility for them.

Disclaimer: Burn Prevention Campaign is not against tea. This campaign is a safety measure that intend to prevent burn injuries in children from hot tea. It is catered to teach parents to be careful while drinking tea.

Any people depicted in stock imagery provided by Getty Images are models, and such images are being used for illustrative purposes only. Certain stock imagery © Getty Images.

This book is printed on acid-free paper.

Writer's assistant: Alisa Ali
Illustration by: Jack Delany

ISBN: 978-1-6655-1978-6 (sc)
ISBN: 978-1-6655-1977-9 (hc)
ISBN: 978-1-6655-1979-3 (e)

Print information available on the last page.

Published by AuthorHouse  06/24/2021

authorHOUSE®

Dedicated to my granddaughter, Izza Effendi,
who helped me create the characters
for this story through her toys.

# This story focuses on preventing scald burns and its first aid.

### Children:

Always stay five steps away from hot liquids.

### Parents:

When you see this mark

practice the prevention with your kids.

Izza woke up early this morning.

Ella, Izza's puppy, and Sonu, Izza's bird, were already awake.

They jumped with joy because grandma has invited them to a tea party!

Izza happily got ready and walked toward grandma's home along with Ella, Sonu, and her mom.

Ding Dong!

Grandma opened the door with
joy and gave Izza a hug.

"Where is Grandpa?" Izza asked excitedly.

"He is reading the newspaper," Grandma replied.

"I'm going in the kitchen to
make the tea," she added.

Izza followed her grandma in the kitchen.

"Grandma, I want to help you," Izza said. She was looking at the stove.

"Kids should always stay five steps away from the stove," Grandma told her.

"Why grandma? Why should kids stay five steps away from the stove?" asked Izza curiously.

"That's because there is a pot on the stove which has hot water for tea. Hot water burns like fire," Grandma explained to Izza.

"Moreover, the handle of the pot should be facing back and the pot should be on the back burner," said Grandma.

"Ok, grandma." Izza nodded her head.

Now Izza knows that she needs to stay

*five steps away* from the stove to protect herself.

Grandma put the tea kettle on the
dining table and said to Izza,

"Tea is ready! I will go get your mom and Grandpa."

As soon as Grandma left the room,
Izza said to Ella and Sonu,

"Let's go and eat the cake! It looks delicious!"

Izza pulled the table cloth to grab the cake!

When Ella and Sonu saw Izza do that, Ella started barking, "woof-woof-woof!" and Sonu started chirping, "chun-chun-chun!"

Hearing the noise, Izza's mom came running into the room and yelled, "Stop Izza! Don't pull the tablecloth! Hot tea will spill and it will burn you!"

"Don't you know that if hot tea spills, it burns like fire? If you get burned the scar from burning never goes away, unlike the stain that can easily be washed away from a cloth, and it is very painful," said Izza's mom.

"Always keep yourself and your friends five steps away from hot liquids," she continued.

Izza promised her family, "I will always stay five steps away from hot tea. And I will tell my friends to do the same!"

# Burn Prevention Activity

Circle the picture that has hot liquids.
And kids should *always stay five steps away!*

# Burn Prevention Quiz

Circle "T" for True or "F" for False after each question

1. Kids should stay five steps away from hot stoves. T or F

2. Hot water burns like fire. T or F

3. Kids should stay one step away from hot liquids. T or F

1. T   2. T   3. F

# Burn Safety Award

Awarded to

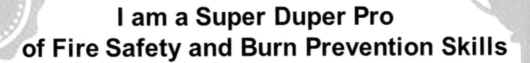

_____

## I am a Super Duper Pro
## of Fire Safety and Burn Prevention Skills

Now I know that
I should Always Stay 5 Steps Away
from Hot Stoves and Hot Liquids.

Super Duper Pro
Award

_____          _____
Pro Signature                                      Parent Signature

Readers now promise
that you will
always five steps away from

# Hot liquids

Proceeds from the sale of *Izza's Tea Party* will go toward providing burn treatment to children all around the world.

10802 Sugar Hill Drive, Suite A
Houston, TX 77042
Tel: 713-266-8002
www.houseofcharity.com
Email: info@houseofcharity.com

# First Aid For Scald Burns

✓ Cool the burn for **20 minutes** with cool running tap water. Seek immediate medical attention.

✕ Do not use ice, iced water, butter, toothpaste, any creams.

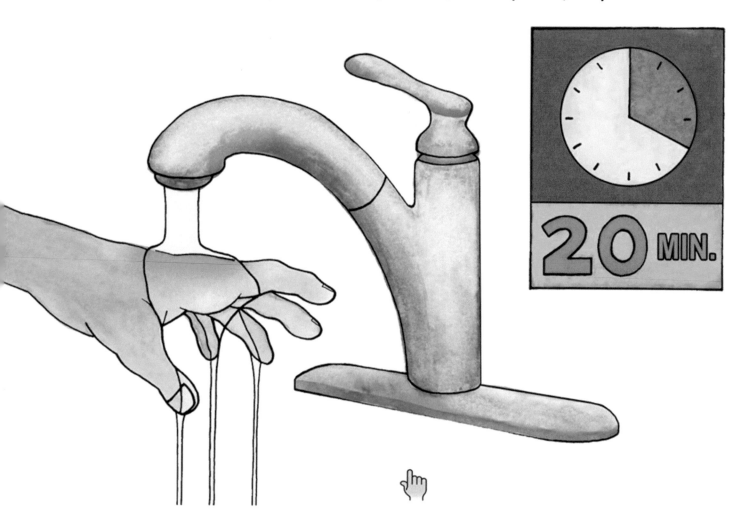

20 MIN.

Printed in the United States
by Baker & Taylor Publisher Services